ANDREA GABRIELI

TEN MADRIGALS

FOR MIXED VOICES

Edited by DENIS ARNOLD

OXFORD UNIVERSITY PRESS
MUSIC DEPARTMENT 44 CONDUIT STREET LONDON WIR ODE

PREFACE

Andrea Gabrieli was born in the sestiere of Cannareggio in Venice probably in the second decade of the sixteenth century. Nothing is known of his early life, but in 1558 he was organist at the Venetian church of S. Geremia, and shortly after this, he went to Munich to enter the service of Duke Albert V of Bavaria, at a time when Orlando di Lasso was in charge of the musical establishment there. He returned to his native city to become organist of St Mark's in 1566 and remained in this post until his death in 1586. He thus spent most of his life in the employ of Duke and Doge.

The nature of his duties naturally meant that a great deal of his music was written for ceremonial occasions of state, and his church music, much of it composed in the polychoral style popular in both Munich and Venice, is mainly conceived on a large scale. In his madrigals, necessarily more domestic, this grand manner can often be felt, even when the resources are more restricted than in his motets. The book of 'Concerti', published by his nephew in 1587, contains several secular pieces for *cori spezzati*, including a number of dialogues for double choir which may well have been part of the incidental music for plays. Other madrigals, notably those in the book of *Madrigali e Ricercari* (again a posthumous publication) were written for public festivities in Venice, such as those in 1571 to celebrate the victory of Lepanto when colourfully decorated floats were pulled through the Piazza. Gabrieli was also a favourite composer of wedding madrigals, where his flair for sonority is put to good use though the resources do not exceed five or six voices. But this is only one side of Gabrieli's nature. He is also the master of the lighter madrigal and canzonetta, having a natural gift for memorable phrases and bright diatonic harmony. Though a follower of Rore in his close concern for expressing the meaning of the words, he never allows this to disturb a sense of musical pattern, and many of his madrigals have repeated sections to give them shape and scale.

The present selection of his work is intended both to provide attractive music for choirs to sing (and choirs rather than vocal consorts are needed by the ceremonial nature of the larger works) and to represent Gabrieli's career at all its stages. *Felici d'Adria* seems to have been written for the visit to Venice of an Austrian nobleman, probably Archduke Charles (1540–90) of Carinthia, whose wife was the daughter of Gabrieli's Bavarian patron, Duke Albert. *Dunque il comun poter* is a hymn in praise of Venice, while *Non vedi o sacr' Apollo* may, as Einstein surmises (1), have been a chorus from one of the classical plays often given before the nobility during festivals. Of the rest, the early madrigals show the preponderance of male voices and of a more contrapuntal approach to the genre, in contrast to later works where the upper voices add lightness to the texture and the century's tendency towards homophony is more strongly in evidence.

In the transcriptions, the time values of the originals are unchanged, since to reduce them would destroy the composer's distinction between *misura da breve* for serious and monumental pieces and the *misura comune* for the lighter works. Although the *musica da breve* logically should result in four minims to the bar and this solution presents no difficulty for *I'vo piangendo*, in the other pieces two minims per bar makes the singers' task easier. The madrigals are also given in untransposed versions. There is no evidence that chamber music pitch in sixteenth century Venice was radically different from our own, and the *chiavette* theories do not apply to these madrigals. As transposition often eases the problems of one voice only at the expense of another, it seems best to leave them as they are. Accidentals in square brackets, cautionary accidentals in round brackets, bar lines, and the keyboard reduction are editorial.

The texts are given in the original orthography with one or two minor changes only to remove awkward spellings which would present difficulty to the singer. All punctuation is editorial. Literal (and thus necessarily inelegant) translations at the foot of the first page of each madrigal are given, rather than singing translations which are nearly always unsatisfactory. The only real difficulty in singing Italian, after the vowel sounds have been learned, concerns elision of syllables, which are frequent in the later madrigals. The solution to this problem is to say the syllables joined together naturally and to try to reproduce their relative lengths in the music. Thus, for example, in *Quando penso* the elision 'ove_amor' might result in two roughly equal vowel sounds, though the one in 'begli_occhi' should shorten the first vowel to obtain a satisfactory declamation.

(1) The Italian Madrigal II

SOURCES

Il dolce sonno: Il primo libro de Madrigali a tre voci, Venice, 1575
   Gardano.
   Verse: anonymous.

Dunque il comun poter: Madrigali et ricercari a quattro voci, Venice,
   1589 Gardano.
   Verse: anonymous.

Vorrei mostrar, madonna: ibid.

Dapoi che su'l fiorire: Il Desiderio, secondo libro de madrigali a cinque
   voci, de diversi auttori, Venice, 1566 Scotto.
   Verse: anonymous.

Quando penso: Il primo libro de madrigali a cinque voci, Venice, 1566
   Gardano.
   Verse: anonymous.

Non vedi o sacr'Apollo: Il secondo libro di madrigali a cinque voci,
   Venice, 1570 Gardano.
   Verse: anonymous.

Angel dal terzo ciel: ibid.

Piangeranno: Il terzo libro de madrigali a cinque voci, Venice, 1589
   Gardano.
   Verse: Petrarch.

I' vo piangendo: ibid.

Felici d'Adria: Il secondo libro di madrigali a cinque voci, Venice,
   1570 Gardano.
   Verse: anonymous.

TEN MADRIGALS

Edited by
DENIS ARNOLD

ANDREA GABRIELI

1. IL DOLCE SONNO

The sweet dream promises me peace, but the bitter awakening takes me back to a state of war; the sweet dream proved false, but, alas, the bitter awakening is no error. If the truth disturbs me and un-reality pleases me may I never hear or see anything on earth; if to sleep gives pleasure, and the awakening pain, may I sleep for ever.

Printed in Great Britain

OXFORD UNIVERSITY PRESS, MUSIC DEPARTMENT, 44 CONDUIT STREET, LONDON W1R ODE

vega mai più ver' in ter - ra, Se'l___ dor-mir mi___

vega mai più ver'___ in ter - ra, Se'l___ dor-mir

vega mai più ver' in ter - ra, Se'l dor-mir mi___

dà gau - dio e'l veg-giar gua - i Poss' io dor-mir, poss' io dor-

mi dà gau - dio e'l veg-giar gua - i Poss' io dor-mir, poss' io dor-

___ dà gau - dio e'l veg-giar gua - i Poss' io dor-mir, poss' io dor-

4

-mir sen - za de - star - mi ma - i, Se'l___ dor - mir mi dà gau - dio e'l

-mir sen - za de - star - mi ma - i, Se'l___ dor - mir mi___ dà gau - dio e'l

-mir sen - za de - star - mi ma - i, Se'l dor - mir mi___ dà gau - dio e'l

veg - giar gua - i Poss' io dor - mir, poss' io dor - mir sen - za de - star - mi ma - i.

veg - giar gua - i Poss' io dor - mir, poss' io dor - mir sen - za de - star - mi ma - i.

veg - giar gua - i Poss' io dor - mir, poss' io dor - mir sen - za de - star - mi ma - i.

2. DUNQUE IL COMUN POTER

for rehearsal only

So through the common power joining together, all share in this happy enterprise. Here the world is upright, here corruption laments its fate, here the liberal heaven displays all its riches; but a man's honour binds him to defend he who has justice on his side, so that the true Gods, meeting each hour, can watch how justice lives and injustice dies.

3. VORREI MOSTRAR, MADONNA

for rehearsal only

I would like to show, my lady, to her who cannot see my heart, how great is the fire with which love afflicts it, nor can I utter a word capable of showing the magnitude of my ardour. But he who wishes to discover how great my ardour really is should look at your beauty; for as it is great, so is the fire in me.

Ten Madrigals

quant' è bel-lez-za_in vo - i: mi

vo - - i: mi - ri vo-stra___ bel-tà___

quant' è bel-lez-za_in vo - i: mi - ri vo - stra bel-tà, mi -

quant' è bel-lez-za_in vo - i: mi - ri vo - stra bel - tà

- ri vo - stra___ bel - tà   che tan-to_è po -

___ che tan-to_è po - i,   che tan-to_è po - i, che tan-to_è

- ri vo - stra bel - tà che tan-to_è po - i,   che tan-to_è

che tan-to_è po - i,   che

4. DAPOI CHE SU'L FIORIRE

for rehearsal only

Since while yet it flowers, I wake to find that hope is dead, what better fate can I have than to die? For that death was ever more sweet and pious because in leaving this life, by grace I shall go (even though I do not deserve it) where my lady, in dying, has gone; and shall know for certain if that gentle soul sees my ardent love from heaven.

5. QUANDO PENSO

for rehearsal only

When I think of that place where with her beauteous eyes love opened my heart, with sweet words caressed it, whence I acquired a so joyous pastime that until the end of my days, I shall always burn, desirous only of renewing myself in her; and already, though suffering so pain- fully, I take pleasure in the sweet memory of her noble manner which can make me completely happy and can so absorb me that I die in her alone, in her I live contented.

Ten Madrigals

6. NON VEDI O SACR'APOLLO

Do you not see, O holy Apollo, how so unjustly this blessed soul languishes, and awaits your help. Come, sweet god, for no human hand
must heal her, who has only offended against the envy of the gods
by her rare beauty and lineage. O what a gracious and good deed would
be yours, if she was protected by you, this blessed soul who so unjustly languishes and awaits your help.

Ten Madrigals

7. ANGEL DAL TERZO CIEL

Angel from the third heaven, descended among us to carry away with you to among the blessed spirits the new Helen, your enchanting bride, behold the celestial fates shower on you the height of happiness; while she has your heart with her, and in you her beautiful spirit is at rest. So in heaven she becomes immortal, disturbed by neither joy, heat or ice.

La no - va E - le - na, tua di - let - ta spo - -

La no - va E - le - na, tua di - let - ta spo - - -

-va E - le - na, tua di - let - ta spo - -

- le - na, tua, la no - va E - le - na, tua di - let - ta spo -

- le - na, tua, la no - va E - le - na, tua di - let - ta spo -

- sa, Ec - coi ce - le - sti fa - ti

- sa, Ec - coi ce - le - sti fa - ti

- sa, Ec - co, ec - coi ce - le - sti fa - ti

- sa, Ec - coi ce - le - sti fa - ti

- sa, Ec - coi ce - le - sti fa - ti

8. PIANGERANNO

The graces weep, and Venus and the Cupids and the one you worship on earth, lucky Grechin, when you die and the sweet tears that fall from their radiant stars for sorrow water the ground where you will be buried, they will yield those green herbs and sweetly smelling flowers which come forth in spring.

Ten Madrigals

Ten Madrigals

9. I'VO PIANGENDO

I keep lamenting my past which I spent loving a mortal, without raising myself in flight, though I had wings with which to show my not too base qualities. You, king of heaven, who see my vile and wicked evils, invisible, immortal, help this lost and feeble soul, and make good its flaws by your grace. So that if I have lived among war and tempest, at least I may die in peace and in port; and if my stay was in vain, at least my departing shall be honest. In the little of life that is left to me, and in my dying, may your hand be near me. You know full well that I have no hope in anyone else.

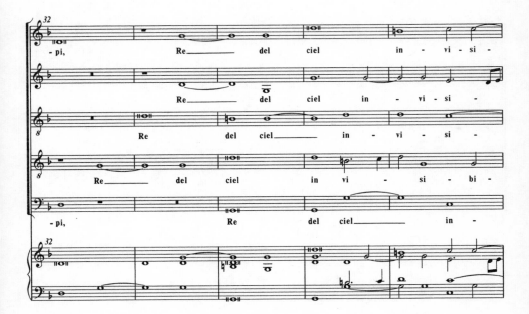

58

Seconda parte

10. FELICI D'ADRIA

for rehearsal only

Happy people of the shores of the Adriatic, for heaven has conferred
on you the privilege of seeing that Nobleman of the house of Austria,
and to raise your voices with the glorious name of Charles, so that
the world may hear how quickly it will come to pass that to his sac-
-red banner Africa will bow, and together all Asia and Europe, intent
on honouring him, will say: Long live the great Charles.